We Leave Gaps

© Alex McKeown 2025

All rights reserved. Except for appropriate use in a book review, no part of this publication may be reproduced, stored in a retrieval system, or transmitted in any form or by any means, without the prior permission of the publisher, or in the case of photocopying or reprographic copying, a licence from the Copyright Agency of Australia.

We Leave Gaps

ISBN 9781763825987

Walleah Press
South Launceston
Tasmania, Australia 7249

www.walleahpress.com.au
ralph-walleahpress@proton.me

We Leave Gaps

by Alex McKeown

Table of Contents

- Gaps...1
- Gift Horses..2
- Strawberry Plant...3
- soaking reminder..4
- qu'est-ce que c'est qu'un sansonnet?.................5
- Classical Poem..6
- Clogyrnach..7
- Doorstep Plea..8
- A Love Poem...9
- A Childhood Birthday Party..........................10
- Young Love...11
- An Introduction To Narratology....................12
- Ubi Sunt Qui Ante Nos Fuerunt....................14
- Confessional Poem..15
- Samsara...16
- When taken as the penultimate acknowledgement that flesh rots..17
- My More Than Human World (Is Here).......18
- Fragment,..19
- Glances..20
- Lights..21
- Layers..22
- Voyages...23
- Jueju..24
- Three Waka of Longing.................................25
- I tried   I tried..............................27
- I'd Have Called Her Sooner..........................28
- ?..29
- Daydream Ascent..30
- Wrenched..31

Writer's Burst	32
schrodinger and his	34
Finally	36
Epitaph for Gough	37
man at the hospital	38
Tanka	39
At the Prison	40
Meeting	41
Smile Though Your Heart Is Breaking	42
Nachtlied	43
Veil (Ghazal)	44
Away (Ghazal)	45
Ghazal Of Your Memory	47
Leaps	48
Alien	49
Dialogue Following Afternoon Tea	50
Gladness At Sadness's Door	52
You're looking for the letter	54
Two Talents	55
Abstraction	57
Hanging	58
Doorstep Thoughts	59
Echo	61
Self Prayer	62
A Kind Of Nature Poem	64
Interview with a Former Major Poet	69
Villanelle	71
Ours	73
prayer for kunanyi	74
Acknowledgements	76
About the Author	77

Gaps

We cannot

leave gaps

,even the ones we need,

free free parking

cannot remain

simply free

for long

we'll fill it in

with our remainders our debts

and anything else except

nothingness which

,perhaps, is too

reminiscent

of emptiness

Gift Horses

The mouth

is not

the problem. Lips

do not reflect. Teeth

hide only phlegm.

But a blank stare

opens lines

of questions

better left.

Never look

a horse in the eye.

Strawberry Plant

she kneels

digs

plants it

and waits

"this time…"

but in her mind

the other times

have grown

too big

the lie

this time

only makes

her sick

soaking reminder

it's been so long

since i swum

since i was young

i'd laugh and splash

soar and spin

and glide and

wish i were

wish i were

wish i were a fish

now bathing upright

in a rushed forgetful morning

i recall the days when i, not time, was short

and my dreams were always soaring

qu'est-ce que c'est qu'un sansonnet?

a sonnetling

who never

grew

to see the fruits

of sonnethood

never soared

from its tree

its wings were cut

before its lines

were said

as others

descend

my sansonnet

is dead

Classical Poem

He was to give himself to me,

Zeus weighed his fate, it fell.

And yet I never drove my blade

Through his fair flesh to spill

The pulsing life, never stripped

The armour from his chest,

Nor would he sigh my name in prophesy

As I'd lay him down to rest.

Caught in his eyes, I baulked at the will

Of Kronos' Son, I left

My prize to fall to another's arms,

And curled in bed, bereft.

Clogyrnach

If you forget me someday dear,

I will forget you, have no fear.

When one magnet dies

its pair falls likewise

though it tries

to adhere

Doorstep Plea

They have a word in Spain

      hasta mañana

Please let me explain

I know I said today, yesterday

Please let me explain

      hasta mañana

They have a word in Spain

A Love Poem

See

how the fable

revives

How the quiet

toad coated

dart flies

From my hand

through

the vent

To you

in your thinly

veiled room

Where you read

what I write

in your head

A Childhood Birthday Party

We're tingling with

a wish for

adventure

The patter

of parents

mingling inside

Drives us

further

towards the stars

Where we'll story

our memories

and become

Who

we

are

Young Love

A certain breeze

was coming

to tell them

they themselves

were breezes

and promptly

they would feel

the regulating force

of self awareness

But for now

sweeping in and out

of windows

they simply lived

as two in love

repeating

whispered phrases which

still whistle

in my ears

An Introduction to Narratology

Adrift in the universe's

implied state

I arrived

on the stage which

Was almost a full course

of fallacies

Scientists declared me

sane but

The institution of

unlimited freedom played

On the narrative soul to hold

in steady intimacy

Discordant discourse which

with infernal inference

Scraped survival from my

supposed interpretation

Ubi Sunt Qui Ante Nos Fuerunt

Where are they who

before us were?

And what would they say

if they still were?

"Hurry on, hurry on,

I can't wait to show you!"?

Or "My God, My God,

Stay away, I implore you!"?

Confessional Poem

My skin is tearing

me from my bones

and my bones are so skinny

and sore

can't you see them?

torn white strips

of pain snapping

away from my

dripping brown

guts

plop plop

I'm all over the floor

I'M ALL OVER THE FLOOR

get me a mop

I'm all over the floor

Samsara

Won't

    I

        be done

  soon?

          A nisus

      sus

  in a noose?

                      No.

                      Debit.

                      Now.

When taken as the penultimate acknowledgement that flesh rots

nothing seems overdone

the calf caressing the thighs

of its mother's lies

the castle built beside the imploring tides

and   though I know that you are mine

the twilit sky

which reminds me of

the closing of

your eyes

My More Than Human World (Is Here)

the starry sky is my

home away from home is more

a quilt around my shivering flesh than

a roof above my head is more than a human

companion in my travels through the world

the starry starry sky is

whispering in my ear i am here

Fragment,

you're too big

additions will skin you

I eye your potentials

I'll kill them

and a poem will live

Glances

i.

dusk

by a blonde smile at the edge

of my eye swiped right

ii.

stinging my eyes

the wind soaked cold

your exasperated sigh

iii.

your lips on his

your eyes on mine

winter mist

Lights

i.

little screen glowing over my eye a space child starry sky

ii.

lamp lit room

bjjshj kshjjk

fried fly wafts

iii.

spiral globe

with a faint green glow

can't you sleep either

iv.

insomnia

a wet summer night's drive

as headlights slip by

Layers

i.

babushka babushka

every year added

further away

ii.

boxing day

thin skinned babushka

dried of tears

Voyages

i.

suburban reserve

here i first met issa

watched the ants wander

ii.

under the branches

of my make-do path

a signpost

iii.

dew on the porch

amazon box

let the pages fall

iv.

windy morning

my pavement shadow

has some crazy hair

Jueju

i.

Cliff walk,   up so high,

Far jazz,   soft, wafts by.

There's joy.   Here's flat peace…

Fox Trot!   Feet shall fly!

ii.

step up   steep stone stair

come down   but take care

my mind   eyes that skirt

she slips   but I'm there

Three Waka of Longing

i.

From Izumi Shikibu

if only the only

first bud of spring

were this first bud of spring

he'd come

through the mists

he'd come

ii.

From Ariwara no Narihira

i'm not sure

if i saw you but spark

or mirage

the sudden flame

that flared in my heart

will kill me all the same

iii.

From Anonymous

the trinket i loved

i hate

it rants and rants

trinket shut up

why won't you

forget about him

I tried   **I tried**

to find the light   but everything's black   when something is nothing
pinhole of white   it's hard to keep track   everything's black

I'd Have Called Her Sooner

Finally I lifted the phone to my ear

And I listened to it ring

>I'd have called her sooner

>But I'd left it so late already

>She'd know how late I was

>How thoughtless and selfish

>To have kept her waiting

>So I waited till I could lie

>And call it sudden

>And I called

It sudden

And so she thought better of me

She thought better

Of me

With her pardoning

Crackling voice on the line

I think she thought

Better of me

?

Could I speak with you?

How awkward to be asked,

to think have I been unmasked…

Could there be a thing more awkward?

Yes. To have them hear

the things you wish and fear

they'll say: to be unmasked.

Daydream Ascent

I'd like to feel the firmament beneath my feet

Some day drown in clouds deep

With rain and rise then fall then rise

Knowing I've stood and so don't need to stand

On heights of heaven's floor, my hand

Free to fall loose or let fly

With force and force myself to floors

More high than I could possibly eye

From ground girt with dirt and pores

Wrenched

You wrench the rhyme I'll wrench the beat

We'll dance through the pain we'll never forfeit

Four feet together though wrenched out of place

We'll drag ourselves over this broken surface

Sureface don't stop though your limbs are tired

This is our battle it's how we are tried

Try hard though you're weak I'll lead through the mess

I'll swing round the mines and make them useless

Use less of your strength make your steps small

It's my turn to lead now you're not able

A ball can be torture when there seems no end

But you've got to hold out and let yourself mend

If you wrench the rhyme then I'll wrench the beat

And we'll dance through the pain on our blistered four feet

Writer's Burst

"I gradually acquired a backlog of unwritten new poems which it took me first weeks, then months, then finally years to get round to"

- Stephen Edgar

Stephen Edgar saves ideas for later selves to eat

I'm too selfish for that, I throw another oyster on my plate

Next month or next I'll starve and wait, starve and wait, and wait

*

In a few years or so

I bet I'll have the gall

To call this a golden age

As if things were going well

Fuck myself, he don't know

*

Thank you Muses for this recent burst

It wasn't us

Then thank you Jesus from the bottom of my heart

    Me it was not

Then Evolution for building me up

    Not I my child

But…

    You sold your soul to the Devil

        and then forgot

schrödinger and his

the cat waited

under its box

it waited

obedient

like a dog

schrödinger lifted the box

the cat was a dog

the dog was soaking

it shook itself off

now schrödinger was soaking

"that's not what I wanted

that's not what I wanted at all

all i ever wanted

was a cat

that was gone and not gone

not a dog"

the dog crept away
wishing it was gone

the dog crept away
sheepishly unzipping

its canine garb
the dog crept away

the dog

Finally.

relief splits me
takes me finally
breathe in   breathe out
in   out
in and out
entirely

Epitaph for Gough

well may we say

there'll be no end

nothing will save

nothing transcend

(posted to Twitter on the day of the death of Gough Whitlam, 21st Prime Minister of Australia)

man at the hospital

he lifts

a bag

like a child

as if it's

a child

he holds it

to his chest

and sinks

Tanka

the reddening face of the child

who watches

other children play

as a grown-up asks

what are your friends' names?

At The Prison

After Guillaume Apollinaire

These hours pass slow

Slow like a burial

You'll weep for this hour of woe

It'll leave us quick

Like all the hours we've known

Meeting

Two cars verge in the midnight rain

They are faltering dent sickened bombs

Don't shine yourself away

All either can see as it moves through its lane

Are the dazzling orbs of a foe

I won't shine myself away

They slip past   close to a touch

And their tails trail in a glow

Smile Though Your Heart Is Breaking

Does he feel unkind who

no longer under duress

lowers his practised smile

alone while no-one sees

Doesn't he feel that he's

depriving us of succour

our gills becoming filled

with suffocating air

Give us

something

something to breathe

Nachtlied

Let's play a round of skat

Let's play a round of skat

We're all alone tonight

So let's play a round of skat

You sit on the left

And you sit on the right

I'll sit here and deal the cards

We're all alone tonight

Drei, skat, vier, und drei

The cards fall all around

And for a time just one of us

Is all alone tonight

Veil (Ghazal)

After Hafiz

The dust of my flesh is to my soul a veil

A joy I'll feel as I uplift this veil

What have you sung sweet song to deserve such cage

To Rezvan fly north, your native home's his vale

Straining to see wherefrom I sail or why

There's pain longing for reason dimmed by a veil

You wish to travel the earth beyond this earth?

Nailed to a tomb your screaming won't avail

Don't stare. The colours of my flickering veil

Hide fires. You don't want the burning behind this veil

Hafiz has lived now breathe his life from him

With you I won't be heard beyond our veil

Based on a literal translation and commentary by Elizabeth T. Gray Jr.

Away (Ghazal)

I'm silent as she rows away

My life, it simply flows away

Layers of lies have enveloped you

Will you let me lift your clothes away?

Father why won't you play? I'm too

Deformed since you stole my nose away?

I know you'll never love me sweet

Yet I can't keep these Os away

I don't want to lose you, I wish I could own you

Take to the bank and close away

You're all my verse, don't be my cage

Don't make me throw my prose away

I kiss only you as we embark

A ghost of her stows away

I don't want to be sad—The Defender Of Men

Is wise, ask him if he knows a way

Ghazal Of Your Memory

Choking at night from a mare of your memory

In a fit of hurt I tear at your memory

I stare. Poems of nothing mist

In the disinfected air of your memory

Little bird uncaged do you

Recall recall am I there in your memory

I thirst you more than time could quench

In a pensieve's juice let me share in your memory

Reader, I was born your slave

Release me from the lair of your memory

Leaps

Only a leap away from oblivion

The freedom only the truly free are given

The ripening apple yearns to kiss the dirt

The blissful moth to merge into the blue

Birds fly. So is the bird who's never flown

A bird? Or just the shadow of a bird?

Leaping from light show to light show at light speed

To blur what we don't want to see: humans die.

But Oh! to dive into a pool of houris

To be a houri in a sea of houris!

To reach the promised land of nothingness

And yet once there to feel no nothingness

We're monkeys swinging star to star waiting

For the sun to rise and let us fall

Alien

i.

You're desperate to

merge into the world

to be your friends

to feel with them

to know

instinctively

what they'll do

to be a part

integrally

a part

of something

beyond you.

ii.

But,

you.

Dialogue Following Afternoon Tea

Why didn't you tell me there was cheese?

I didn't know.

You knew.

I didn't know you cared.

I did.

But I didn't know.

Were there biscuits?

Yes

And fruits?

Yes.

                                    Strawberries?

                    Yes

You knew.

Gladness At Sadness's Door

Hello Sadness!

    Hello Gladness…

You're looking… je ne sais quoi *today!*

    Oh Gladness…

    Oh Sadness!

I'm afraid I can't come out today…

    The sun is bright, the sky is blue
and all is good in the world!

But last night

    it was night

  the end of the light…

                           Ah, night…

Gladness please!

    I can't come out today

        Why not? Why not today?

Gladness, I'm still grieving

    for yesterday

You're looking for the letter

From Lionel Ray

You're looking for the letter, lost

with the wandering words,

you're looking for a name in an elsewhere

that's nowhere.

The forest in the bird

the voice in the silent

the far in the near.

But you are your own measure,

so little of day, so little of night,

Suspended between the source and fire,

Enmeshed with incestuous plants.

You're the buried flame

who no longer recalls　　　　　　　except

a face like a shadow's grain.

Two Talents

July 2012

It's been twenty-four years

And my light is spent

On the first

Eight hours a day

And I can't get to sleep

With these songs in my head

I wrote them a year ago

And then an hour ago

Sat up and feared

They were gone

(Since when was the last time

I sat and played? Just played?)

And how can I know

But to go through them all

Singing upside down

The songs that were once mine

And lined my mind

Every day with space and light

I had the space to play

The light to write by

And now they're spent

The first eight hours a day

Abstraction

I can almost squeeze

the juices from tomorrow

sip the almost bitter

could be sweet next week

but sometimes my grip

loosens my tongue numbs

I know but cannot hear

the agonised pleas

of the venomed future me

his tears are tasteless

like the blood of glaciers

dripping to the sea

Hanging

by a thread

the spider grips its bug

blood is running to its head

and from my bed I can hear the shell

cracking

but gravity is always pulling

dizzying the spider's grip

so now that bug is

falling

imagine the expression

of the spider slowly seeing

and all its little feelers

slowly reaching then

realing

Doorstep Thoughts

If I die today will I become lost

in the waste of your childhood reflections

thrown away with the meals and the toys that break

and the murky morning dreams?

Will my care my love and warmth collapse into oblivion?

As I watch you play with your puzzle games

curled up in your little blue chair talking with your favourite bear

as I'm about to leave and say goodbye I stop

and think: what if you never hear me again if this is our very last kiss?

Am I held together enough to keep?

Or will you cling desperately

as the pieces fall

away

until one day

you wake

up

      with a

      nagging thought

      that

      there's

      something

      you've

          forgotten

      something

                        important

Echo

when winter comes

we'll think of you again

be warmed

by the sunlit flames

of your eyes

and nourished

by the wonders

of your lips

    like that lazy mouse

    who saw the beauty in the sun

    and the leaves and the fruits

    when they were there

    and remembered them still

    in winter

        when winter comes

        we'll think of you again

        be warmed

        by the sunlit flames

        of your eyes

        and nourished

        by the wonders

        of your lips

Self Prayer

Let them free, the walls, the fools
    in the holes, the whole five volts
        as the bell's on hold

Let them free, the eyes, the slides,
    the sliding tides and the hiding child
        in the scarecrow rides

Let them free though they know,
    they only know, but don't go also,
        just let them free

Let them free, the people you keep
    in the deep and all the teething heaps
        that seep

Let them free, the laughing jacks,
    and the jump-in box and all the clocks
        wound back

    Let them free

        and be free

            of all you've seen

                of all you've been

be free

A Kind Of Nature Poem

Cento from Gina Mercer's collection of ecopoetry weaving nests with smoke and stone

Scotch, no ice, for her,   driest red for him.

They have drunk their fill,   faces lifting,

Passing the binoculars   back and forth,

Scanning the small   horizon for inattentive flesh.

They are spare winter   savaged and pared.

There's Little Red   Riding Hood!

Plaits afuzz   in the afternoon air,

Oblivious   to the bustle of dangers,

Lying luxurious   all anyhow

Coloured royally   crimson and blue

In some high-rise   aluminium apartment,

Shrugging off her hood   stripping down to slightly.

A body so compact   a car designer sighs,

A curving tail of such symmetry   a sculptor's fingers twitch.

They sip and toast   each other,

Take their own   watchful time.

He is mindful of her hips   as they swivel and dip,

His pearly pot belly   drift-dancing,

Fig opulent skin   stretched pregnant.

She, still railing   strong against

Her compact completeness,   her questing eye,

Clucks her sonnet   of contentment.

Swivelling slow   as interstellar radar,

No haste, no chase,   no ache-needing,

Firm as any high   priestess hairdresser,

She drops suddenly   on delicate thread,

Full length, lustrous,   joy-tight serpent

Around the arc   of hip sockets.

Gently she chirrups   calling down the sweet swoon,

Soft cooing to soothe,   claws to slit open,

Mimicking the cries   of a lost kitten,

Until trans-   spiration releases them.

Each drop takes   its task seriously.

The walled green   world goes hush,

Throwing whoops of orange   up to the white ceiling.

Brushing elbows   and lips after,

Music bathes   the light rich room.

They sing acapella with   the daffodils

Into the darkling deep   ocean of dream.

For once they are   silent, intent.

Strong sharp   shapes contrasting,

I find my hair   begins to flick:

I want to clasp each   one in tender hands.

All the birds   in my brain fly out.

Oh to be a swamp   snake now

Out in   odd places

Coiling fearless tendrils   through furled anatomy!

Feeding on   the flourishing lawn

Creamy trunks   girdled by metal teeth.

To murmur secrets   each to each

In the dark brown   itch of evening,

To atomise, stir, to glisten   inexorably up!

How hard it is   to make my mind,

(Aclatter with   jitter and clutter,

Hectic with electronic mating   and high-speed slumber)

Nest amid   the rectangular ridges,

Full of grass and sky.   The grey mice of anxiety scuttle in

Plaguing and creeping   tussock to tussock

Across the aching   afternoon.

"Forget all you know   about Canute The King.

Breathe shafts of sun   into the winter bathroom.

Lie on the sand. Open   everything to the sun.

Imagine the exquisite   apparatus of your kidneys.

See these paperbarks   leaning languid

On a remote reef   perched out in the Pacific.

Gaze at the diving   gannets. Become one."

Even following   such strictures

Why all the embarrassment about   being happy?

It's tough weather for flying: wings won't hold

Dictated by that eternal   task master, gravity!

Rain decorates,   soaks my shirt.

I step, feckless,   my feet tasting,

Feeding on   the flourishing lawn.

I see Little Red Riding,   hood out, walking

In her grey-blue   size-too-big blazer.

Tonight she'll tip   toe a halo,

Softly following   a pair of rosellas

Up into the valley's   spiralling air.

Soaring is perhaps   not effortless…

---

* The line "Why all the embarrassment about being happy" was written by Wendell Berry and reused by Mercer

Interview with a Former Major Poet

What was it like to be a great, to be
A king amongst your peers? It was a fine

Thing to know they thought so much of me,
That all the schools were scanning every line,

But most to know I'd live through history
In dialogue with greater minds than mine.

So it was hard then, when it came? The decline?
Yes. Could you speak a bit about it? Fine.

There was a fairly gradual shift you see,
As my contemporaries died, replaced by fresh

And eager minds, my words no longer breathed.
They saw the world in different hues to me

And shared perception's all a poet's let;
We build with words and words can move, they're free

To dance and love whichever way they please.

Some of your peers retained their stature — Yes.

I guess they may have held a more timeless…

No… universal mode of thought to me.

So that's it then? You're doomed to second rate?

Perhaps. The only thing to do is wait

—*For what?* Perhaps I'll be remembered yet,

Reclaimed by some ambitious child who sees

What poets saw in me to name me great.

Things change. I'm proof of that. No man knows his fate.

Villanelle

I weep for but I shun the dead

Who creep in shadow, creek in wind.

The house is filled with things they said.

The remnants of a life once led

Are scars upon the left behind.

I weep for but I shun the dead.

And when I turning lie in bed

They move conversing through my mind,

A house that's filled with things they said.

I find some memories I dread

To lose, and some I dread to find.

I weep for and I shun the dead.

Instead of hearing their dark tread,

I'd like to vanish, deaf and blind

Like the house that's filled with things they said.

O once my villanelle's been read

And they come to my side, remind

Me: *weep for them but shun the dead,*

Your house is full with things they said.

Ours

Living in a damp and empty hole
we hold precious what is ours
even if it's forks of twig
and dried out dirt in our mouths

And if that dirt is just for us
and our neighbours' trees have none
then maybe we shall feel some pride
in our poorly selves for once

And can you really blame us then
if our neighbours call to us
"you'll never guess what we just got,
some dirt to fill us up!"

We feel more poor than ever before
and so creep up their tree
to find that little bowl of dirt
and throw it in the sea

prayer for kunanyi

If the mountain feels uncomprehended

let it know that its every nook

has been seen sometime by somebody

that even a favourite book cannot be savoured whole

in one moment though each word

is a gift and each page an adventure.

Let it not forget

we remember all of its silhouettes

from north, south, east and west, since it

means home to us and home,

no matter how long estranged,

stays learnt by heart.

If the mountain feels the urge to stray,

frustrated by its own immensity and commitment

to an unwavering position, let it recall

we all take it with us on the plane,

through us it has seen glaciers

canyons, skyscrapers, the depths

of the oceans and breadth of the deserts.

If the mountain in winter fears that its icy exterior

makes it seem cold-hearted and hateful,

feels that our eyes are filled with bitter contempt

when a breeze blows through its snows into us,

let it recall the icy palm

of love on the infant's fevered brow

and that warmth is only felt through knowledge of coldness.

If the mountain is lonely

let it bask in the brightness of the sun, find solace

in the spirit fumes of the moon:

these two will always be there for you.

And know that though we may struggle

with our lives and be restless and sometimes leave you

we will come back to you.

Acknowledgments

Most of the poems in this collection were written on the lands of the Muwinina people.

Thanks are due to following outlets for initial publication of poems: *Island Magazine, Southerly Journal, The Canberra Times, Cordite Poetry Review, Plumwood Mountain Journal, Australian Poetry Journal, Snorkel, Otoliths, fourW, The Ghazal Page, Right Hand Pointing, paper wasp, Coolabah, Seven By Twenty, World Haiku Review, Penteract Press, Bluepepper, Ezra: An Online Journal of Translation, Echidna Tracks, Riddled With Arrows, Authora Australis, Magma, Windfall: Australian Haiku*

"My More Than Human World (Is Here)" was written as part of the *More-Than-Human Poetry Project* and performed as a round at The Hobart Writers Festival.

About the Author

Alex McKeown is a 36-year-old Tasmanian writer and software engineer.

He has published widely in Australian outlets including *Southerly*, *Australian Poetry Journal*, *Island*, *Cordite*, *The Canberra Times*, *Plumwood Mountain* and *Transnational Literature*. He is also a writer of haiku, which have appeared in *Echidna Tracks*, *Windfall*, *paper wasp*, *World Haiku Review*, and the Haiku Foundation's *Haiku in Australia* anthology. His chapbook of translations from the French of Antoinette Deshoulières, *Love In The Fields*, appeared with the UK's Penteract Press in 2022.

Alex has been active in the writing community, appearing at Seasonal Poets, The Hobart Writers Festival, and the National Young Writers Festival, has given workshops for young people with TasWriters, and judged the Tasmanian Poetry Festival's Andrew Hardy Youth Poetry Prize in 2023 and 2024. Alex is slated to be among the featured poets performing at the Tasmanian Poetry Festival in Launceston this October 2025.

More of his writing can be found at:

alexmckeownpoetry.com

instagram.com/alexmckeownpoetry/

www.ingramcontent.com/pod-product-compliance
Lightning Source LLC
Chambersburg PA
CBHW020546080526
44583CB00013B/1023